PENPALS *for* Handwriting

Year 6 Practice Book (10–11 years)

By **Gill Budgell & Kate Ruttle**

Supported by the
National Handwriting Association
Promoting good practice

Contents

CAMBRIDGE
UNIVERSITY PRESS

Practise the joins.

th   ti   tr   ta   tt

Same letters, new join. Try it.

th   ti   tr   ta   tt

Write these words then rewrite them with the new join.

attraction   *competitor*

hospital   *theatre*

restaurant   *committee*

Do you prefer joining from the baseline or from the cross bar? Why?

Speeding up
Rewrite at least three times using your chosen join at an increasing speed:

*the travelling
trapeze artists*

Check:
- the join from *t*
- the consistency of the join when
  you write faster.

Find one join from *t* **to tick and two
to improve.**
Rewrite them.

**Write the words using
your chosen joins.**

train station

leisure centre

cafeteria

taxi rank

art gallery

history museum

2

Try joining from *g*.

gl   gi   gr   ga   gg

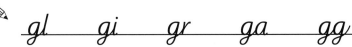

Write the words using your chosen joins.

Write these words then rewrite them with the new join.

edge   *angle*

diagram   *regular*

tangram   *bigger*

maths game   *algorithm*

geometry

biology

geography

graphics

Which join do you prefer? Why?

Speeding up
Rewrite at least three times using your chosen join at an increasing speed:

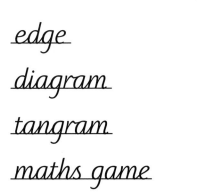

giggling girls
began to juggle

Check:
- the join from *g*
- the consistency of the join when you write faster.

Find one join from *g* to tick and two to improve.
Rewrite them.

technology

trigonometry

3

Try joining from *j* and *y*.

je   jo   ye   yr   yo

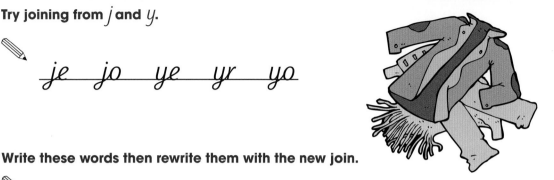

Write these words then rewrite them with the new join.

jacket

jeans

jogging bottoms

jeggings

cycling helmet

yoga trousers

gym kit

jazz-dance leotard

Which join do you prefer? Why?

Speeding up
Rewrite at least three times using your chosen join at an increasing speed:

eight yaks went

jogging in yellow

pyjamas

Check:
- the join from *j* and *y*
- the consistency of the join when you write faster.

Find one join from *j* and one from *y* to tick and two to improve.
Rewrite them.

> Write the words using your chosen joins.

jewellery

jumpsuit

lycra

enjoyment

jockey silks

yachting jacket

Practise the joins.

 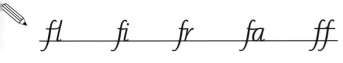

Same letters, new join. Try it.

Write these words then rewrite them with the new join.

- football
- off side
- defence
- offence

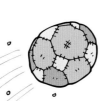

- first team
- free kick
- final score
- referee

Which join do you prefer? Why?

Speeding up
Rewrite at least three times using your chosen join at an increasing speed:

fifteen footballers
followed the referee

Check:
- the joins from _f_
- the consistency of the join when you write faster.

Find one join from _f_ to tick and two to improve.
Rewrite them.

Write the words using your chosen joins.

flick

official

front row

hopeful

fearful

performance

5

Practise the joins *us, us, uɔ*

enthusiastic
enthusiastic
enthusiastic

Write these words then rewrite them with the new joins.

Join 1 *us*	Join 2 *us*	Join 3 *uɔ*
blissful		
stressed		
cautious		
upset		
confused		
isolated		

Which join do you prefer? Why?

Practise the pattern.

Write the words using your chosen joins.

basic

frustrated

uneasy

insecure

disappointed

compassionate

Check:
- the joins to *s*
- the consistency of the join when you write faster.

Find one join to *s* to tick and two to improve.
Rewrite them.

Practise the joins.

bl   bu   br   ba   bb

Same letters, new joins. Try it.

bl   bu   br   ba   bb

Write these words then rewrite them with the new join.

bath

beauty

bubble

cotton buds

bath robe

emery board

hair brush

cabinet

Which join do you prefer? Why?

Practise the pattern.

Check:
- the join from b
- the consistency of the join when you write faster.

Find one join from b to tick and two to improve.
Rewrite them.

> **Write the words using your chosen joins.**

blue

brown

beige

auburn

ebony

burnt umber

Practise the letters.

v	w	x	z
v	w	x x	3 3

Write these words then rewrite them with the new joins.

Join 1	Join 2	Join 3
gazelle		
aardvark		
beaver		
swordfish		
oxen		
wolf		

Which join do you prefer? Why?

Practise the pattern.

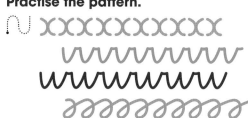

Check:
- the joins to and from v, w, x, z
- the consistency of the join when you write faster.

Find one join to tick and two to improve.
Rewrite them.

Write the words using your chosen joins.

whale

vixen

vulture

zoological

aardwolf

chimpanzee

Write the heading.

Abbreviations

Write down what the teacher says in note form. You do not need to use your best handwriting, but it must be legible.

Please remember:
Be at school by eight forty-five because
we are leaving on the coach promptly at
nine o'clock. You will be on the coach for
over three hours so bring something to eat
and drink. We will return to school by three
thirty. You may bring a bag, a telephone
and no more than five pounds.

Practise the pattern.

Check:
- if the notes included the key facts
- which words you abbreviated.

Find one word to tick and two to improve.
Rewrite them.

Write the words using your chosen joins.

morning a.m.

afternoon p.m.

more than >

less than <

et cetera etc.

example e.g.

9

Write the tips for serving. Use joined, sloped handwriting.
Make sure your words are equally spaced. Use your preferred joins.

Tips for serving in tennis

1. Stand on the baseline.

2. Don't throw the ball up too high.

3. Try to throw the ball up slightly
in front of you.

4. Aim to hit the ball with the centre
of the racket head.

Practise the pattern.

Check:
- your spacing
- you have left 1–2 letter *o*s
  between each word.

Find one example of well-spaced
words to tick and two to improve.
Rewrite them.

Write the words using
your chosen joins.

tennis ball

tennis court

racket head

tennis net

serve and volley

match point

10

Write the words at speed. Time yourself.
Use your chosen joins and personal style.
You must be quick but your writing must still be legible.

Write the words using
your chosen joins.

1. hospital restaurant
2. geography diagram
3. yachting jacket
4. fantastic performance
5. upset and stressed
6. absolute bubble bath
7. aardvarks, oxen and whales
8. Abbreviate at, and, example.
9. Spacing between words is important for clarity.
10. Letters must be evenly spaced and consistently sized.

choice

personal

selection

style

purpose

etcetera

Practise the pattern.

Check:
Write your preferred join for each pair.

to	to		so	so	oo
g	go		y	yo	
fa	fo		v	v	w	w
j	jo		x	x	z	z

11

Write the heading. Keep the letter sizes as shown. Write the descriptions.

OLD FASHIONED FOOTBALL STRIPS
Arsenal: red and blue stripes
Bolton Wanderers: white with red spots
Coventry City: black shirts
Everton: salmon-pink shirts
Leeds United: blue shirt with yellow trim
Liverpool: blue and white halves
Newcastle United: red and white stripes
Watford: red, yellow and green hoops.

Check the letter sizing: width and height.

Speeding up
Rewrite at least three times using your
chosen join at an increasing speed:

Consistent sizing
makes writing easier
to read. True or False?

Check:
- that your capitals are the same
  height as your ascenders
  (except *t* which is a little shorter).

**Find one word to tick and two
to improve.**
Rewrite them.

**Write the words using
your chosen joins.**

Chelsea

Aston Villa

York City

Manchester City

Southampton

Tottenham Hotspur

Write the heading. Keep the proportion as it is shown here.

Capitals same height as ascenders.

The Digestive System

Descenders same height as ascenders.

Write the information. Check the proportion.

The system breaks down food for the body to absorb. It travels like this:

mouth ----▶ *oesophagus* ----▶ *stomach* ----

----▶ *small intestine* ----▶ *large intestine*

Practise the pattern.

⌒

xdxgxt

Write the words using your chosen joins.

skeleton

muscles

blood

body

nutrients

intestinal

Check:
- that, within letters, the ascenders, bodies (x-height) and descenders are of equal proportions. This means letters will be similar in both width and height to each other, which makes for easier reading.

Find one word to tick and two to improve. Rewrite them.

Write the heading. Keep the letter spacing as it is shown here.

An Acrostic Poem

Leave equal spacing between letters in a word.

Leave 1–2 letter *o*s between each word.

Now write the rest of the poem using the letter spaces as shown.

A favourite literary devi
Ce is the one whe
Re the first letter
Of each line spell
S out the subject the poe
T wishes to write about.
I must admit, I
Can't see the point myself.
Roger McGough

Rewrite it now as a running text.

Speeding up
Rewrite at least three times using your chosen join at an increasing speed:

jolly jingles and
humorous haiku

Check:
- spacing within words, between words, between lines of writing
- layout and the use of blank space on the page
- consistent spacing makes writing easier to read and looks better.

Find one word to tick and two to improve.
Rewrite them.

Write the words using your chosen joins.

poems

classics

jingles

kennings

haiku

sonnets

Write the heading.

Check the ascenders are all a similar height to each other and to capitals.

Keep the ascenders and descenders parallel as shown here.

Greek Gods and Goddesses

Now write your own heading to include some letters with descenders.

Now write this information. Correct all errors of ascender and descender sizing.

Demeter: goddess of farming
Hades: god of the underworld
Zeus: king of the gods

Write the words using your chosen joins.

myths

legends

democracy

civilisation

mysteries

Mount Olympus

Speeding up
Rewrite at least three times using your chosen join at an increasing speed:

Apollo is god of music, poetry and light.

Check:
- the sizing of ascenders and descenders
- the parallel lines of ascenders and descenders
- legibility.

Find one word to tick and two to improve. Rewrite them.

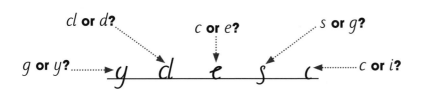

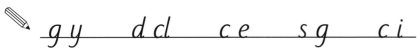

Practise writing these letters.

g y   d cl   c e   s g   c i

Sometimes writing at speed leads to poor quality letters or joins.

Write each phrase twice; once slowly and once at speed to see what happens to your writing.

an excellent disguise

an allergy to sugar

an accident with a biscuit

a circle on the ceiling

declaring innocence

Practise the pattern.

Check:
- your writing for any loss of quality to open and closed letters.

Find one join to tick and two to improve.
Rewrite them.

> **Write the words using your chosen joins.**

technology

energy

deciding

practice

biscuit

classifying

We can make decisions about when to use a pen break in our writing.
This impacts on fluency.

Write each word with and then without breaks.

abom in able
abominable

snow man
snowman

anti dis establish ment arian ism
antidisestablishmentarianism

super cali frag ilistic expi ali docious
supercalifragilisticexpialidocious

cir cum fer ence
circumference

en vir on men tal
environmental

app rox i mate ly
approximately

Practise the pattern.

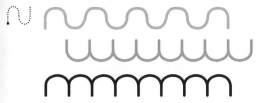

Check:
- if you preferred using pen breaks.
  If so, why?

Find one word to tick and two to improve.
Rewrite them.

Write the words using
your chosen joins.

literature

dramatically

autobiography

adventurous

fascination

independence

Write the heading. Keep the letter spacing as it is shown here.

Annotations

Write the haiku in your best handwriting. Write the annotations in quick note-making handwriting.

simple idea

5 syllables line 1

Scooping up water:
The moon in my hands ripples,
Fingers open, gone.

strong image

7 syllables line 2

Add at least one further annotation.

Practise the pattern.

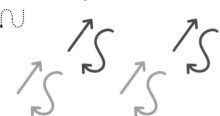

Check:
- that your annotations include abbreviated words
- the readability of your quick note-making handwriting.

Find one word to tick and two to improve. Rewrite them.

Write the words using your chosen joins.

letter

word

syllable

syllabification

simplicity

impressionistic

Write the heading. Keep the presentation as shown here.

 Environmental Issues

Write this sentence for each of the different situations below.

 We can protect the environment in many different ways.

- for a caption on a display board

- for a heading on a poster

- for a test answer

- for self only in a notebook

- as part of an art display

Practise the pattern.

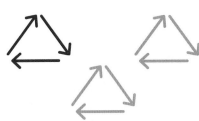

Write the words using your chosen joins.

purpose

audience

legibility

font

style

impact

Check:
- you have chosen a suitable style for each situation
- with a partner why we may choose different styles.

Compare and discuss your different handwriting choices with a friend. Explain each choice.

It's important to choose the right tool for the task. This may include using technology to create a handwritten or stylised effect.

Match a writing tool to each task below. Write out each choice, e.g.

I'd probably use a crayon (E) for a colouring-in book.

- a handwritten invitation
- decorative edging to a picture
- for a colouring-in book
- a formal hand-written letter
- some rough notes
- working on a whiteboard

A

B

C

D

E

F

Practise the pattern.

kkkkkkk
sssssssss

Check:
- your choices. Compare with others' choices.

Try some!

Write the words using your chosen joins.

pencil

paint brush

marker pen

crayon

felt pen

fountain pen

Write these instructions. Use your chosen joins and personal style.

Handwriting Reminders

Check:

- the height of your CAPITALS in relation to your lower-case letters
- the proportions (roundness, height, length, width) of your letters
- your letters are spaced evenly in a word
- the relative size, length, height of ascenders and descenders
- your open letters are open and your closed letters are closed
- you can write long words without taking a pen break
- your hand is moving smoothly over the page
- you can use different styles or standards of handwriting for different purposes
- which style you are using for this activity. Why?
- you can select the right tool for the task.

What are these handwriting issues important?

What is your next target for improving your handwriting?

Do you have two or more styles or standards of handwriting? e.g. best, quick, fancy, rough.

Do you know which tool to use for different tasks?

Add one of your own instructions.

Write the biographical information at speed in joined, sloped writing as if for a timed test.

Henry MOORE
1898–1986
British sculptor

Moore studied at the Leeds School of Art, Yorkshire and the Royal College of Art, London. By the 1940s, he had achieved international recognition.

Now write the same information for a display.
Use print letters (straight, unjoined, no exit flicks).

Compare the two versions.

Speeding up
Rewrite at least three times using your chosen join at an increasing speed:

'The observation of nature is part of an artist's life.' Moore

Check:
- capital letters
- lower case letters
- numbers
- punctuation
- joins.

Find one word to tick and one to improve.
Rewrite them.

Write the words using your chosen joins.

artist

graphic

sculptor

jeweller

potter

carpenter

Write the heading.

Note Making

Make notes from this passage about the Amazon River. Use your quick note-making handwriting.

The world's largest rainforest grows in the basin of the mighty Amazon: the longest river in South America. The Amazon rises in the snow-capped Andes in Peru then flows six thousand, four hundred and thirty-nine kilometres to its mouth in the Atlantic Ocean.

Make a fact file about the Amazon River. Use neat handwriting.

Practise the pattern.

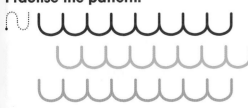

Check:
- the legibility of your notes. Can you read them?
- the neatness of your fact file.

Find one join to tick and two to improve. Rewrite them.

Write the words using your chosen joins.

jot

note

flag

annotate

summarise

proofread

Write the heading.

Neat writing; Super Scribers

Imagine setting up a business in the future that offers THE very best handwritten messages.

Write the advert in your very best handwriting to entice new scribes to join your business.

Do you love handwriting as much as we do? Maybe you should become one of our specialist scribes? At Super Scribe, all our letters are handwritten by our talented, reliable and script-perfect writers. Do you love to share your expertise? Could you be one of our Super Scribers?

Write the words using your chosen joins.

note

crafted

scribe

inscription

precision

wordsmith

Practise the pattern.

ee ee ee

tt tt tt

pp pp pp

Check:
- the neatness of your writing in the advert
- legibility
- the slope
- the joins.

24

Write the following personal information. Use your clearest print lettering.

Write the words using your chosen joins.

Zane Boyband
10 Star Boulevard
Fametown
Supershire
SK1D 5BN

Tel: 44(0) 1598 730253
Mob: 07381 534996
www.zanebb.com

symbols

print

sloped

joined

Now write your own address like this.

Practise the pattern.

Check:
- your print letters are upright and clear
- symbols and numbers are clean.

Find one word to tick and two to improve.
Rewrite them.

numbers

style

25

Write out each description for the different styles of writing.

Note making: quick writing, often including abbreviations, which needs to be legible to the writer only.

Fast and fluent writing: the most useful style of handwriting. It must be neat and legible to all readers.

Best writing: only used for presentations. Likely to be slow and careful. Appearance and legibility are paramount.

Printing for presentation: used for labelling, captions, posters, etc.

Provide an example of handwriting to match each style described.
List other styles you like to use.

Speeding up
Rewrite at least three times using your chosen join at an increasing speed:

Fast and fluent writing is the most useful.

Check:
- each description
- each description works for its purpose?
- all descriptions legible?

Find one word to tick and two to improve.
Rewrite them.

Write the words using your chosen joins.

styles

fonts

italics

bubble

formal

presentation

Write the heading.

✏️ *Calligraphy*

Copy this calligraphy. Then write the text in at least two other ways.

✏️

Calligraphy
This word is from Ancient Greek :
kallos beauty and graphe writing.

Practise the pattern.

ꡫ *n n n n*
n n n n

Check:
- the flow of your letters
- the legibility
- if your style is joined
- if your style is sloped or upright.

Find one word to tick and two to improve.
Rewrite them.

> **Write the words using your chosen joins.** ✏️

visual art

lettering

design

flat-edged pen

round hand

italic

We use different lettering for different purposes.

Write these decorated capital letters. Consider which tool is best for the task.

They are the same height as the alphabet capitals but they may be extended above or below the line.

ABC
DEF
GHI
JLKM
NOP
QRS
TUV
WXyZ

ABC
DEF
GHI
JLKM
NOP
QRS
TUV
WXYZ

ABC
DEF
GHI
JLKM
NOP
QRS
TUV
WXYZ

Write the words using your chosen joins.

grapheme

graphic

gothic

illustrated

medieval

modern

Practise the pattern.

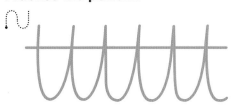

Check:
- the proportions of the double letters
- layout.

Find one letter to tick and two to improve.
Rewrite them.

Write the heading.

Instructions

Write this paragraph as a numbered list. Use sloped, joined handwriting.

To make Rocky Road you need to line a baking tray. In a large saucepan melt some butter with chocolate and golden syrup until there are no lumps. Put crushed biscuits, marshmallows and any other delicious ingredients into the chocolate mix. You should stir it all up and tip it into the tray. Spread it all out and put it into the fridge for about two hours.

Write the words using your chosen joins.

instructions

recipe

coding

directions

model-making

guidance

Practise the pattern.

Check:
- your layout
- your slope and joins.

Find one join to tick and two to improve.
Rewrite them.

Write the text in your own style that matches its purpose.

 A book review

Title:

Author:

Publisher:

ISBN:

- Why did the cover/blurb attract you?

- What are the strengths of the book, in your opinion?

- What are its weaknesses?

- Would you recommend this book?

- Who do you think might enjoy it?

- Have you read any other books by this author?

- Would you read another by this author?

Now complete the review for a book you are reading.

Then use the questions on p31 to self- or peer-assess your handwriting.

Use these questions to self- or peer-assess your handwriting. Award a mark for each 'yes'.

Letter formation
Are all your letters formed correctly?
Which letters do you form in more
than one way?
Are any letters closed which should be open?
Are any letters open that should be closed?

Joining
Check three examples of each of these joins:
- diagonal join, no ascender
- diagonal join to ascender
- diagonal join to an anticlockwise letter
- horizontal join, no ascender
- horizontal join to ascender
- horizontal join to an anticlockwise letter.
Which letters do you join in more than one way?
Which letters are consistently break letters?

Proportions
Are all the letters on the baseline?
Are the lower case short letters all the same size?
Are the ascenders in proportion to the rest
of your writing?

Are the descenders in proportion to the rest
of your writing?
Are capitals consistently sized?

Spacing
Are spaces within words consistent?
Are letters too close together or too far apart?
Are pen breaks used appropriately in longer words?
Are spaces between words consistent?
Are words too close together or too far apart?

Style and presentation
Are you using different styles of handwriting for
different purposes?
- Note-making
- Fast and fluent
- Best handwriting
- Print
- Capitals
- Interesting lettering and decoration

**Now select a piece of writing from a different
subject and repeat the assessment.**

Draw these patterns and self-assess your skills.

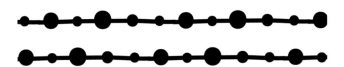

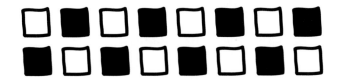

Check:
- patterns are repeating
- patterns are evenly sized
- patterns are copied accurately.